Najee K. Carter

THE WORLD THROUGH MY EYES

**ON A MISSION NKC LLC
"THE WORLD THROUGH MY EYES"
WWW.MYSPACE.COM/CARTER303
P.O. BOX 206
BLOOMFIELD, NJ 07003-0206
Feel Free to Contact
TEEN Author NAJEE K. CARTER**

NAJEE K. CARTER

Bloomington, IN  Milton Keynes, UK

AuthorHouse™
1663 Liberty Drive, Suite 200
Bloomington, IN 47403
www.authorhouse.com
Phone: 1-800-839-8640

AuthorHouse™ UK Ltd.
500 Avebury Boulevard
Central Milton Keynes, MK9 2BE
www.authorhouse.co.uk
Phone: 08001974150

© 2007 Najee K. Carter. All rights reserved.

No part of this book may be reproduced, stored in a retrieval system, or transmitted by any means without the written permission of the author.

First published by AuthorHouse 4/16/2007

ISBN: 978-1-4343-0579-4 (sc)

Printed in the United States of America
Bloomington, Indiana

This book is printed on acid-free paper.

Table of Contents

Acknowledgements	vii
The World Through My Eyes Introduction	1
World Through My Eyes: Last In The Race	3
Inspiration: The World Through My Eyes Last In The Race	5
The Man That I Am	7
Who Am I?	9
I Am You	10
Dreams	11
Agony and Pain	13
Najee	14
Sweet 16	15
Inspiration: The World Through My Eyes (Sweet 16)	17
True Friends	19
Lust or Love	20
Title: Sweet Sixteen (story)	21
I Am The Missing Link	28
Get Away	30
4 Drops Of Tears	31
Emotionally Corrupt Individual	32
Am I Capable Of Love	34
Hip Hop	35
Inspiration: The World Through My Eyes Hip Hop	37
Imminent Destruction	39
Flaws	41
"Get Over It"	42
Lynches Poison	43
Inspiration: The World Through My Eyes: Willy Lynch's Curse	45
No More Lies	47
So Many Tears	48
Spiritual Warfare	49
Who Are You?	50
Double Minded	51
Counterfeit Christian	53
The World Through My Eyes: On A Mission	55

I Can Now Fly	58
New Beginnings The Beginning Of A New Man	59
Voice Of The Ghetto	61
Victim Of The Streets	63
Why Kill What We Made	64
Grandma's House	65
Education And Basketball	67
It's So Hard To Say Goodbye	69
School, To Me, Wasn't Cool	73
Tomorrow Is Not Promised	75
The Supposed Oppressor	77
My Mission	79
I Am The Future	81
Can I	82
You (No One In Your Corner)	83
To My Oldest Son, Najee	85
Innocent Child Left	87
Time Out To Meet The Author	91

ACKNOWLEDGEMENTS

FIRST AND FOREMOST, I would like to thank my Lord and Savior Jesus Christ for giving me the gift of poetry so that I can share my journey with the world. If it were not for my relationship with him I would have not been able to surpass the storms of my life. Whenever I feel completely abandoned and alone the lord is there watching over me. I couldn't imagine my book being successful without me giving credit where credit is due. I like to describe my poetry as being the voice of God speaking through me. It is he who gives me the strength to overcome my trials and to now share my story with the world.

To my mother, Tangela Brown, I thank you from the bottom of my heart. Words could never explain my love for you. You have been the greatest inspiration in my life and I truly love you. Only my actions could possibly show how you have so positively influenced my life through your strength, courage, and unconditional love. To my grandmother, Flora Motley, I thank you for introducing me to this candid form of expression called poetry. I thank you for always believing in my ability and for showing me that all things are possible through Christ who strengthens me.

To everyone back home in New Jersey, I thank you for your support and appreciation of my art form. I'd like to thank those at Bloomfield High school that remained true to me, "Da Homiez". I love you from the bottom of my heart and pray that you all live your dreams. To everyone with a dream I just want you to know that where there is a will there is a way. I would like to inspire you to never be afraid to attain your goals. I must also thank my ancestors, those who have lost their lives so that I can reap the benefits of freedom.

To anyone who has taken the time to read my book I would like to show my most honest and sincere gratitude. It is truly a blessing for me to be an inspiration to someone else. Words could never explain how grateful I am to be given the opportunity to share my story with the world. I would like to thank everyone that God has sent my way to help me on my journey. I thank everyone who has truly loved me and believed in my ability. Lastly, I would like to thank anyone who told me that I couldn't because that only pushed me to be even stronger.

Love Najee Khabir Carter

The World Through My Eyes
Introduction

The World through My Eyes is my way of expressing my feelings about growing up as a teenage African-American male in a society governed by norms and expectations. Growing up in a single-parent home with violence and temptation surrounding me makes my perception of the world different from that of the typical American family. I view the world as being a place filled with evil and destruction with our only means of survival being God's love and mercy. Throughout my times of sorrow and pain, it is he who keeps me safe in a world plagued with violence, drugs, wickedness, and counterfeit gods.

As a child, I always was captivated by the beauty of words and their different meanings. Whenever I heard a word that was foreign to me, my inquisitive nature would always persuade me to find out its meanings. Although I always had this love for words, I did not start writing poetry until I was thirteen years old. This was a time in my life when the poison of insecurity heavily polluted my very being. I found out at an early age that I didn't fit the African-American community's image of normal because of my very dark skin tone. It was only until I hit the pre-teenage years that this insecurity held me captive. Poetry to me at first was a way of escaping the reality that for all of my life I would be ridiculed simply for who I was. It later evolved into a way for me to face the reality that I would have to love who I am. As my writing ability grew, I felt myself growing, and it is still a journey I am on.

I have been blessed by the genes of an exceptionally talented bloodline. My grandmother, who is one of my greatest inspirations, is a multitalented poet, singer, songwriter, and artist who gave birth to singers and poets. It is through her genes and the genes of those who came before her that I have the ability to write. Most importantly, my ability comes through God's anointing. When I was younger, I recited her poetry at school events and talent shows until I discovered my own gift. She introduced me to an untraditional form of poetry that comes from the heart. It is through God-sent people like her and my mother (who is my strongest encouragement and my backbone) that I can say I have surpassed the storm.

It would be selfish to say that my poetry is my voice, because it is the voice of God speaking through me. The reason I write is to help both others and myself to overcome the trials and tribulations that we face while here on earth. I speak of freeing yourself from the chains of insecurity, hate, animosity, and envy. I also speak of fighting the temptations of this world. Most importantly, I speak the truth. I speak the truth about how our society was built to keep the best interests of the elite few. Throughout my book, you will walk my journey of finding who I am, and you will see the world through my eyes.

World Through My Eyes: Last In The Race

From birth I was placed last in the race

Made to believe that my whole race was a disgrace

In this Land of Freedom and Opportunity

I have to speak "properly" to get a taste of social equality

It's a struggle for me to be all that I can be

When more likely in jail than college is where statistics would place me

But I have decided to go against the grain

Nothing can hold me down, not even the ethnicity of my name

I learn only the sugar-coated half of my past in the history books

History is repeating itself if you just take a look

The policeman are our overseers, and the government our masters

The so called American dream is all that I am after

From the time of my birth I was placed in this international race

Unfortunately, for me, I was put in last place

Just another ethnic name and skin that reads nigger

But I want the whole world to know that my heart, my soul, my dreams, and my aspirations are so much bigger

No longer will "ghetto" or "thug" be my identity

Agree or disagree, but I am addressing these issues candidly

I long for genuine equality and emancipation within our nation

To grow as a nation we must first come to the realization

That coming from the inner -city places me behind in the race for success

Especially when a negative image is placed upon me by the media and the press

Honestly, what do you think when you see me

The stereotypical uneducated, ignorant, violent African-American male minority

Or a human being, and a intellectual with a mind of creativity

A child of God who is going to let my light shine

Through poetry so candid and so divine

An educated black man who will rise from the oppression

Finishing this race with joy as my only expression

I can't help to notice that three fingers are pointed back at my face

Because I don't have to settle for last place

Inspiration:
The World Through My Eyes
Last In The Race

The poem "Last in The Race" means so much to me. The true fact of the matter is that the stereotypes and expectations around being an African-American male mentally place you behind in the race of life. The race to be successful, respected, and treated as an American. I don't want anyone to think that I am pulling the "race-card" by saying this, but this is simply reality. Being an African American automatically gives you a bad reputation. When I enter stores and have the owners look at me closely it hurts my soul. I know my moral standards but all the store owner sees is my skin color. In his mind I can only be a drug dealer or a gang member. And if I want to be successful, I have to be a rapper or athlete. There is so much more to me as an African American. I am intelligent, and I have so much to offer the world.

What I am saying in this poem is that I don't have to be what stereotypes try to make me. I can rise above being last. I don't have to do it illegally. I can go to college and be successful. Being from the ghetto doesn't make me what society considers "ghetto." Only I can control my destiny. If we can get to the point where we overlook race, we as a society will thrive. Each nationality in America has something so special to offer in the formation of our culture. I don't want to be looked at as ignorant or violent because I am Black. I want to be recognized for the contributions that I have made to society. I want to be recognized for the strength of my ancestors who came to this country as slaves. The strength of African Americans who participated in the civil rights movement is who I am. The creativity of all those who were apart of the Harlem Renaissance is also who I am.

What I want all people to get from this poem is that people can only oppress you for as long as you let them. Although it may be more difficult for an African-American to be successful in America, it isn't impossible. The day we learn to stop blaming others for our failures is the day we will rise above the oppression and truly be free. The day that we can stop judging others based upon their outward appearances and learn to love their soul is the day that we can truly live in unison and grow as a world.

The Man That I Am

I can't even look in the mirror when I'm uncomfortable in my own skin

So I hide from myself and neglect the voice within, because

Insecurity has claimed victory over my confidence and sticks closer than a friend

And walking around with my head down has become my own personal trend

I just can't learn to love who I am, and I understand that the clothes don't make the man

So why do I feel it's a necessity for me to wear my clothing name-brand

And when I look into the mirror the name-brand clothing obscures my face

So in this case, it's sad to say but the clothes do make the man

But I just don't understand why I can't love who I am

I long for a layer of confidence that will protect me from the poison of deadly words

The words that make me want to curl up in a ball and die, and then I ask myself why?

Why should I believe this lie that I just may not be good enough for the rest of humanity?

And I believe the lie, because sticks and stones may break my bones

And in this lifetime words will surely hurt me

Potentially killing my pride and every trace of comfort inside, making my confidence hide and therefore yielding my insecurity

Killing my interaction socially this kills me emotionally

But then deep inside where Jesus and my confidence reside, he helps me grow fruitfully

Carrying myself gracefully no matter what others think of me

You see to be assertive is the key, now understanding that I don't have to live to the expectations of humanity, In fact I'm special because the clothes don't make me God makes me. So when I look into the mirror it is an image of him that I see

So why should I walk around with my head down wearing a frown when I am a child of the man who wears the supreme crown

Now the clothes don't make me and harsh words no longer break me

Humanity's norms and boundaries no longer shape me, and it's all because I found love

And oneness with self that I just can't gain anywhere else, and when I don't fit the world image of perfection I give this ignorant world a correction

Beauty is a state of mind your opinion verses mine, See your words could either bring me down like hair with a trim or uplift me like a spiritual hymn, But that's only when I listen to them. Your words no longer make or break me and no longer will material things make the man. Now my integrity, loyalty, respect, self-love and relationship with God define who I am.

Who Am I?

Who truly am I because these feelings I can no longer hide.

Who Am I spiritually, physically, and mentally?

I need to get to know myself a little more personally.

I need a bit more confidence in me,

and always look at myself as beautiful

No matter what others see.

Reaching inside to pull out the best leaving behind all the rest

Always being the best that I can be.

Knowing that I can do all things through Christ who strengthens me.

Not fearful of carrying myself just a bit differently.

Always keeping it real with me, never being what they call phony

Who am I as I study my school books religiously?

Knowing that only I can define my destiny.

I no longer have to squint my eyes to see

The answers were imbedded in my soul deeply.

Always encouraging teens to find themselves.

The journey truly starts at the age of 12.

Peer pressure and trying to fit in, yea

the teenage years are when the saga will begin

Never letting stereotypes or statistics define who I am.

A new journey of **self love, respect and knowing who I am** has just begun.

I Am You

I am a reflection of you and what you put me through
When I look at you I see me, and when you look at me
You see a harsh reminder of yourself
You claim the positive traits but abandon the negative
But I am the mirror image of you

Whether it be a portion of your past or the present life you live
I am a reflection of you and what you put me through
What I know, I learned from you
Whether my knowledge is negative or positive it is attained from you
Through you I have learned culture, and the norms of society
I have learned to love and I have learned to hate

It is through you that I have learned right from wrong
Respect, dignity, confidence, and integrity
Before you scrutinize me closely realize that I am a product of you
The trials and tribulations you put me through
They make me the strong person that I am
Those trials and tribulations are what makes me a man

It's so easy to find the bad in a person
But I am a reflection of you and What I've been through
The obstacles I face the issues I resolve
The opposition I survive, is the way you've taught me to survive
Through me you are alive, and I am you

Dreams

Is it that I think I'm too good to settle for life in the hood?

Or is it that I have dreams that tell me I'm too good

Or am I being so quixotic that I can't even acknowledge that

I can't be the first African- American President

Why? Because my family has no history and I'm not an Ivy League graduate

But those are the lies inside my head wishing that my dreams were dead

So I'm going to go for my dreams so that those lies can never be fed

See dreams are a positive start because they give you something to work for

It's just those lies that say dreams are unrealistic that you have to ignore

Is it that you can't acknowledge or is that you just refuse

To live a life without change is what you choose

Who? Those who tell me that dreams are unrealistic, those who feed me with lies

Those who think that the only way for me to Rise is to compromise

Forget where I come from and delete memories of my past

But it's that past that helps better my future so those memories have to last

Those who frown down upon me and like to see me fall

They can try to bring me down with lies but I continue to stand tall

Like those that came before me I refuse to move

So you can choose to hate but I can't relate, because I chose to win and never lose

What? Lose my motivation and drive that keeps me alive, and enables me to survive, and to strive to do my best, passing the test ending with a testimony

One that is real and not phony

And when it's all over I can say that I've conquered the storm

Surpassed society's norms withstanding the harsh rain with only wisdom to gain

From the ignorance of others I am now redeemed

All because I Dreamed!!!

Agony and Pain

Agony and pain agony and pain.

Go outside and cry to integrate the tears with the rain.

You have only your self to blame.

Tossed away all in life that you had to gain.

Put shame on your name.

Cry away all of your agony and pain.

But don't just wait for the rain.

Let your emotions just go.

That is one of the best ways to deal with issues you know.

Don't hold issues inside for them to later blow.

Don't make the same mistake over again

Next time learn and grow.

Najee

Never letting stereotypes or statistics define me or my destiny.

Assertive, confident, but never egotistical is what I strive to be.

Journeying to understand myself physically, mentally, and spiritually.

Ending my journey by killing any insecurity.

Every thing above this E is a little portion of me.

Sweet 16

Sweet 16 never knew that her body was a temple, and she was its queen

Never realized the beauty she possessed because others were mean

She waited for that day for her prince to take her away, but that was all a dream

All she ever wanted was acceptance, and to be respected

She was sick of being ridiculed, disrespected, and neglected

So she turned to the opposite sex to feel loved and have attention

She threw away her morals, and didn't follow her intuition

She wore clothes that were too short and tightly hugged her curves

Now she was being treated in a manner that not even a dog deserves

She thought it was love but she was being treated like a piece of meat

It was her own insecurity that she would have to learn to defeat

Sweet 16 never knew that her body was a temple and she was its queen

The way she was allowing herself to be treated was unacceptable and obscene.

By the second semester of school she was 3months pregnant

People called her a whore

But I understood that behind the revealing attire there was so much more

She mistook her obsession for love; she thought he was her lover

But reality hit when he left her to be a teenage, single-mother

She never realized that you can't gain self-confidence from someone else

Because self-confidence is a special love for ones self

Inspiration: The World Through My Eyes (Sweet 16)

I WROTE THE poem "Sweet 16" while thinking of a situation that happens all to often in the inner city and all across America. When a young girl is faced with low self-esteem she looks for love in the wrong places. She might look to the opposite sex for that attention. Instead of being loved she is often times being exploited. If you stay in a relationship when you aren't being treated properly it isn't love, it is low self-esteem. A person who loves them self will not allow themselves to be emotionally abused and physically used. When a teenage girl feels that she has to look outside of herself for love, she will often allow the opposite sex to abuse her mentally, mistaking her obsession for love. When a child comes from these relationships many times the young girl is left to be a single mother. Dreams of getting a higher education and pursuing a career are usually tossed away.

Parents should make it their jobs to embed confidence in their children's heart before the world can give them a negative view of themselves. Most of the time if a child has learned confidence from home, it is harder for others to break that confidence. Make it your duty to tell your child every day that they are beautiful, handsome, wonderful, intelligent, loved and special. This way you know that you did your job, in making your child feel secure in his/her appearance, life and ability.

True Friends

True friends are special and their friendship is genuine

When obstacles come your way you can depend on a true friend

They are always there when you need someone to listen

And they truly care about the person within

A true friend has your best interest at heart

When trials come your way, from you they will not part

A true friend's motives are positive from the start

This is why true friendships are God's works of art

Sometimes a true friend can also be a true pain

But the important part is that true friends will always remain

You must first be friendly in order to have friends

Whether or not you will receive true friends really depends

A friend is like a mind, a good one should never go to waste

Just make sure you realize that a true friend is hard to replace

If one would like to consider themselves a true friend

Always remember that a true friend is true to the end

Lust or Love

When you're stimulated sexually but abused mentally
It isn't love you're just confused emotionally
Your head spins when you hear that name
Brain-washed and lost in a childish game
Confused is it love or lust, Deception or trust
It's an infatuation or similar to a chemical equation
So much of your love put in but you get nothing back
Leaving your heart broken and you're mentally attacked

Holding on because you believe you can't let go
Thought that you were loved but little did you know
Robbed of your heart, emotionally torn apart
From the start there were clues, but lust had you confused
Now you're mournful and sad, stressed and a mess
Distinguish lust from love and you will be blessed

Title: Sweet Sixteen (story)

On July 24, 1990, a hot and humid summer morning, Momma gave birth to me, Imani Lewis. My mother was only sixteen years old, and unfortunately, this was a generational curse that wouldn't end here. Adoption was an option, but my mother's young and immature mind led her to believe that I would be the reason for the guy she loved to love her in return. She was dead wrong.

My mother was in no way ready to take on the responsibilities of having a baby. While she was out searching for love in all the wrong places, I was often neglected. It wasn't fair that I should be held responsible for her actions, but it was my reality. How could a child placed in such a horrible situation ever make something of herself?

As a young child, I often traveled with my mother from house to house and city to city. This unstable environment was in no way healthy, but Momma didn't care. She was too selfish to look into my eyes and see my pain. As far back as I can remember, I hated her for the life she gave me. I hated her for being irresponsible.

We lived in Brooklyn, New York with an aunt of mine for a small portion of my childhood. My mother would sometimes run off to stay with a boyfriend who lived in Jersey. As a child, I wasn't as fortunate as my peers. I didn't dress as nicely as they did, and I would definitely have to suffer. I would also be ridiculed for my nappy hair and dark complexion. This began the breaking of me.

Having a poor relationship with my mother only made it easier for me to be scarred by the comments my peers made. I was slowly becoming weaker and weaker. Slowly but surely, I was becoming enslaved by the opinions of others. To make matters worse, when I turned on the television, I didn't see girls that looked like me. How was I ever to believe that I was beautiful?

Never Good Enough

It seemed as if I was never good enough for my mother. She would make it her job to tell me how ugly I was. These statements, made by the lady who gave birth to me, scarred me for life. I was always ugly and unintelligent in her eyes. If only I could have seen my inner beauty. If only I could have believed in the intelligence that I possessed.

It was difficult enough to deal with my peers tormenting me, but imagine coming home to someone who made you feel like nothing. I honestly believed that I was worthless and had nothing at all to contribute to the world. I don't know what my mother's motives were for belittling me, but I think she was also insecure with whom she was. Whenever I was told by my mother that I was ugly, I just couldn't help but notice that I was her reflection, or as some say, the spitting image of her.

During my middle school years, I felt my self-confidence declining even more rapidly. I was always the victim of someone's hateful comment. I didn't understand that people were just jealous. How else could a person take time out of his or her day just to talk about me? I sometimes felt so weak that I thought life couldn't go on. I just couldn't see the light of day. It was difficult for me to believe in myself when I was told so often that I was nothing.

Sixteen Ain't So Sweet

On July 24, 2006, I turned sixteen years old. Some girls throw lavish parties celebrating this wonderful stage of their lives. There's even a show that focuses on sweet-sixteen parties thrown by the super rich. No amount of money could have bought me happiness. The fact of the matter is that I felt ugly. In the eyes of the world, my hair was too short and my skin was too dark. I hated who I was. I desperately just needed someone to love me. Unfortunately, I would search for love in all the wrong places.

My sixteenth birthday was just like any other day of my sad and lonely life. No gift in the world could have filled the void and emptiness that I once felt. My insecurities were slowly but surely killing me off. I didn't feel pretty, and since I didn't feel that way about myself, no one else felt that way about me either. It's amazing how a person's words can damage you deeply and scar you for life.

The scars that my mom left on me from childhood were only growing. Without the love and support of my own mother, I felt alone in a harsh world that wouldn't make me feel any better. Her hateful words damaged my soul. It hindered my ability to move forward and took away from who I was.

Being broken down in my own home only made me even more vulnerable to the world outside. I wished that I had a solid foundation and the support of my family. My insecurities eventually led me to be highly depressed. I often contemplated suicide. It isn't easy going through life hating yourself. Without love for self, you are merely a slave to the thoughts and opinions of those around you. I longed for freedom and acceptance. There were nights when I just lay on my pillow and cried until I couldn't cry anymore. For me, sixteen wasn't so sweet because I still hadn't learned to love me.

Back to School

When September arrived, it was back to school for me. I was now a junior in high school, and I was determined to succeed. The first day of school is always fascinating because you see friends that you may not have spoken to during the summer. It was also fascinating because my gear was "fresh to death." Or at least in my eyes it was. It wouldn't be long before someone would say something about my clothing that would tear away any sense of self-confidence that I may have had. Once again I allowed myself to be the victim of others' ignorance and stupidity.

By walking around with my head down and displaying such low self-esteem, I made myself an easy target for others. If only I had been more confident in myself and my appearance, others would have noticed it. I drew negative attention to myself by displaying such weakness. We live in a cruel world that attacks at the first sign of vulnerability, and I, unfortunately, often became the victim of those attacks.

I was always an intelligent young lady who did rather well in school. After all, my intelligence was all that I had to get me to the next level in this world that's so focused on physical appearance. I started the year off focused on getting good grades and trying to prepare for college. This goal would soon be transformed into a wrongful search for love from the opposite sex. When a member of the opposite sex even noticed my presence, I would feel beautiful. It is sad that I needed someone's insincere attention in order to feel that way about myself.

Promiscuity

After my first sexual experience, I felt loved. It was foolish of me to feel this way, but my longing for acceptance played tricks on my mind. With every touch and kiss I felt loved. Once again I was only the victim of my own vulnerability. My search for love led me to be highly promiscuous. I allowed myself to be degraded and disrespected. I didn't care that others would call me a whore; I just became infatuated with the thought that someone could even be interested in me. I guess I just never understood that to a male it was only sex, and nothing more. I feel for young ladies whom I often see resort to lives of promiscuity. The world views them as disgusting, but I understand that there is a story behind this behavior.

By December of my junior year in high school, I had to deal with the consequences of my promiscuity. I was pregnant. When my mom found out, the first thing she said to me was that I was little whore. She didn't understand the hurt and pain she had caused me. No one understood my pain and the hate I had for myself. My foolish attempt to find love left me pregnant and, once again, alone. I hated being a statistic and a part of the generational curse that has long haunted my family. I hated myself for being so foolish. I wasn't loved; but reality hit when I was left to be a teenage single mother.

I had to develop the strength to go through my junior year of high school while bearing a child. I was ridiculed, talked about, lied about, and everything else. I had no one to blame but myself, even though I was so greatly saddened by the ignorance of others. I had goals and dreams, so I decided that I wouldn't give up on them just because I was pregnant. I instead decided that the life that was growing inside me would be my drive and motivation.

Healing

One day while crying and beating up on myself for the mistakes I made in life, I decided to listen to some music. Music was therapeutic and healing for me. While listening to "Private Party" by the beautiful India Arie, I began to finally understand. I had to learn to love me. I needed time away from everyone else so that I could heal the long-term disconnection that I had from myself. I needed to be strong for me and my baby. "My body is beautiful and sacred and I'm gonna celebrate it," the song says. By listening to this song, I was inspired to not be afraid of who I was. I decided that I needed spiritual healing.

When I think of how beautiful and sacred my body truly is, I wonder how it was ever possible for me to allow myself to be disrespected and treated like a piece of meat. I didn't realize until hearing that song that my body is a temple and I am its queen. Learning about and understanding my beauty was only the beginning of the healing process. Although it wasn't easy, I knew that in order for me to survive and to be strong for my little one, I would have to learn to love me. When you love yourself, you won't allow yourself to be disrespected in any way. I finally understand my true beauty.

It is very important to understand that you must first love yourself. In order to love yourself, you must love God, because God is love. My body is God's temple, and what he has blessed, no man shall curse. I will no longer allow myself or my temple to be corrupted again. I have finally learned to love me.

I Am The Missing Link

Over 500 years lie behind my tears
Triumph and joy suffering and pain
Repetition of history again and again
Enough degradation to drive a whole people insane
But my people sustain, through my ancestor's spirits
That nurtures my heart and my brain

So I'm not your stereotype nor am I your expectation
Like oxygen to blood or a prescription to a patient
I am the very soul to this nation

So don't depreciate my contribution or belittle who I am
For I am the very wealth of this land
I ain't ya cotton pickin nigga expected to pull the trigger
Go to jail raise hell be a statistic and nothing bigger

It would behoove you to acknowledge
My indispensable wisdom and knowledge
I have dreams that surpass the gardens of this state
Enough love to spread from the Brick City to Kuwait

I define my destiny and I determine my fate
Adjacent to he whom no man can equate
Black and beautiful Empowered and spiritual
Intelligent and fearless, Wise and vigorous

I am the missing link because you refuse to accept me
The mystery behind the ebony led you to reject me
Fear of the unknown took royalty from their thrones
And placed them in a land where they were less than a man

Could you even fathom the thoughts of those who were caught and brought
Reduced like fractions unaware of the pale man's actions
Constantly made inferior but that was only the exterior
Because internally they were invincible

With the faith of a mustard seed they even
Conquered the slave owners greed
And that very spirit of invincibility survives eternally
With the faith of a mustard seed no man can conquer me

So call me the new millenniums Moses
Because I am here to give us freedom
Through candid,
Real, heartfelt, and God given poetry

Get Away

Sometimes I feel I gotta get away because this pain is killing me
I feel like the world is against me and I'm standing alone
I feel like this storm of frustration and confusion will never end
The rain of negativity pours heavily on my soul
My spirit is weakened and my mind can't properly function
I desperately need to get away to a place in my mind where I am free
Free from cultural norms, expectations and all negative energy
Where the whole universe pauses on my command
And the world actually revolves around me

Although this may sound highly selfish it's just truly how I'm feeling right now

4 Drops Of Tears

1 drop, 2 drops, 3 drops, 4
Lord please stop the tears from falling because I just can't cry anymore
Tame this beast in my mouth because I just can't lie anymore
Make me hot or cold because I can't be lukewarm anymore
Make me single-minded because I just can't be unstable anymore
I am now older so childish things must come to an end
Make me right Oh Lord, and deliver me from sin
Teach me how to love an to be a true friend
I wanna love more than just my own blood and kin
In your house of prayer I shouldn't dare
play church as a game, use your name in vein
Hypocritical is something that I will never be
Thanks to you from bondage I am free
I will enter your gates with thanksgiving, and into your courts with praise
Shape me, mold me, Lord rid me of my worldly ways

1 drop, 2drops, 3drops, 4
Lord Oh Lord I now cry tears of joy
You no longer have to stop the tears
Dear Lord you've kept me through all of my years
Joyful tears I now cry since the Lord has entered my life
I can live knowing that everyday is a test, and I will do my best
I will trust in you forever, faithfully worshiping your name
For you are an awesome God, and forever you will reign

Emotionally Corrupt Individual

As I walk this green mile quickly approaching my death
I look back over my life, and how I've never been blessed
Have I ever been truly loved, first have I ever been truly hugged
Have I ever been truly kissed?
When I leave this earth will I even be missed?
Man thinking about my life got me pissed
I was never on Santa's good boy list
I sit in this chair almost in tears
Thinking about what happens after death leaves me surrounded by fears
I've never had someone who truly cares

This just ain't right, but I had no right to take that mans life
But see misery loves company, so if I have nothing to live for
You got nothing to live for
Now I'm not giving an excuse for the reason I kill, but this is how I feel
For those who criticize me, If only you knew
If I were raised like you I wouldn't even think about doing half the crap I do.
Even though it's hard to, try putting yourself in my shoes
But you can't can you?
Do you know how it is to feel abandoned since you were two?
You don't know what it is to be an emotionally corrupt individual

My momz was addicted to that powder prostituting every hour
Popz was a deadbeat a no-show and a coward
When I was older I changed my last name from Howard
Felt like I never got love, not even from above
So hate, envy, and violence is all that I could think of
You see Jack and Jill ran up a hill

But I had to see my momma die from that pill

Now I'm not giving and excuse to why I kill, but this is how I feel
My uncle was absolutely delusional
Want to know how it feels to have your own blood abuse you
Your grandmother not claim you, your aunt hate you
But see you don't know what it is to be an emotionally corrupt individual
Abandoned since you were two, love and family is what you knew
This is why you don't do what I do,

So don't judge me take a walk in my shoes
But still I had no right to take that man's life just because I wanted his chain
Now I'm ashamed, I should've also changed my first name
But see I have only myself to blame

Am I Capable Of Love

Can I be patient, and am I capable of being kind
If I can't, should love even be on my mind

Will I be able to trust someone, and never give up
Or will my relationships be disasters and just go corrupt

Will I learn to give up my bragging ways and learn not to be rude
Or will I forever be evil, mean-hearted, and crude.

Can I learn to be unselfish, giving without expecting
Or will my relationships consist of me continually neglecting

Will I ever learn to not easily become angry, and not to argue
Or will I try to play love as a game like others do

Will I always be honest and true just like Jesus above
Or will I always tell lies and be unfaithful, am I capable of love

Hip Hop

Hip Hop, it started out something so real

Something so ill that the soul could feel

Now you have people getting rich off of irrelevant issues

Too afraid to face reality so instead the youth is abused

Come on Hip Hop tell me something I'd like to hear

Stop making this music something that society will fear

Please Oh Please stop glorifying the Ghettoes

While you're in a mansion and your girl is in stilettos

Your music has a world wide impact so use it to your advantage and educate me

Honestly, the majority of what you're doing is filling my mind with stupidity

But see I give credit to those who discuss politics, religion, culture, and history

Unfortunately, those who discuss the negative things put all rappers in a negative category

Use your popularity to create unity within the human race

Do something more useful than adding violence to this already cruel place

Now everyone wants to be either a gangster or a pimp

There's less individuals cuz everyone wants to walk with a limp

Why do catastrophic events have to occur for us to come together

Spend your time wisely because we don't live forever

Stop selling sex without selling reality

Now in school next to me there's a walking STD

Why must you use beef to sell records, talent alone should do that

The problem is we have a whole bunch of rappers who can't rap

Let Hip Hop be real, coming straight from the heart

If all you can do is discuss negativity, then don't rap, and that's a positive start

Inspiration:
The World Through My Eyes
Hip Hop

When I wrote the poem "Hip Hop" it wasn't because I was against the music. It is simply because of my love for the music. I consider hip hop to be a whole sub-culture and a way of life. I would like to see more talented artist becoming successful. I see so many rappers who sell music off of having a hot beat or a catchy hook. It feels as if there is too much negativity being shown in rap music. We call our women so many names that are degrading. It isn't right. It seems like there is only a few topics to discuss. I know that there is so much more happening than violence, sex, and stupidity. I feel with the popularity that rappers have they should use it to better our community. Many rappers lived a life that led to being a thug, gang member, drug dealer, or criminal. By glorifying this way of life on television, you are introducing that life to people who don't have to live that lifestyle. There are people coming from homes with good parents, people who never had to struggle. These people want to be gangsters because it is what they see on TV. The more violence is discussed, believe it or not, the more violence we will have in our communities. If you took a minute and stepped out of the black race, how do you think others view us? We call our women sluts and hoe's instead of beautiful Queens. When a rap battle takes place it should never go any further than that, verbal war. Other people must look at us like we are violent, disrespectful animals.

I believe that artist like Nas, 2pac, Lauryn Hill, Common, Kanye West, and DMX deserve so much respect. Each of these rappers discusses what goes on in the ghettoes of America, but they also have something positive to offer. They discuss religion, history, politics, or culture. I believe people take the easy way out by trying to sound gangster or by discussing their fortunes. We can fight for positive recognition through our music. We need to stop all of the ignorance. Some may say that it isn't their fault, but how do you expect to be famous without being a role model. When you achieve that level of fame you automatically have young children looking up to you. Because of my love for Hip Hop music, I don't want to see it go down the drain, and that's tough love.

Imminent Destruction

Weapons of Mass destruction causing corruption
Political leaders in need of spiritual instruction
Poverty and starvation plague the worlds we call third
While scientific geniuses continue to refuse God's word
Celebrities idolized while minds are being terrorized
Baptized in the water, in need of the fire
Whole congregations deceived by religious liars
Oblivious to truth, lies capture the youth
A generation of sex, drugs, and STD's
Loving fantasy while incarcerated mentally
Young minds mistaking lust for love and denying their maker
Foolish partaker, of fleshly pleasure
Not realizing that we are powerful beyond measure
Defeated by temptation, malice polluting nations

Individuality subliminally being devoured by the norms of humanity
Personality slowly but surely being enslaved to normality
Prosperity rapidly decreasing due to lack of individual diversity
Fearing social rejection we conform for what we believe is protection
Dangerous perception of fear of rejection in need of correction

Senseless tradition as foolish as superstition
Generational curses as if generations rehearse this
Money glorified God's kingdom denied
Youth misguided by what TV calls reality
Lack of truth is the new millennium's poverty
Violence, Drugs, And HIV eradicating the black community
Even after the 13th Amendment we're still in slavery
In too many instances when the majority rules

the majority are fools who choose to lose

Discrimination divides a nation, multiplied by hate
imminent destruction is society's fate
Suicide and mass homicide, nowhere to hide
Oppressed by fear, redemption is here

Poverty and war, incapable of peace
Violence and crime at a major increase
Questions left unanswered and still no cure for cancer
Theories of Big Bang forgetting the King's name
Human rights violated, minds discombobulated
Now can you relate, equate, shall I demonstrate
Ignorance at high rates, senseless debates
As I wait to see science escape societies imminent fate

Flaws

Don't try to fix them, embrace them
Don't try to hide them, flaunt them
Don't try to change them, learn to love them
Don't cry over them, instead smile
Don't let others make you feel bad about them
Show others their beauty
Look in the mirror everyday and say "Looking pretty good today"
I am beautiful; I am handsome, wonderful, intelligent, and unique
I am SOMEBODY!!!

"Get Over It"

Some say get over it
As if it were as simple as 1, 2, 3
Like it was a minor issue that could easily be resolved
How can I simply get over being told I am inferior for so many years
How can I get over having my language and culture ripped away from me
Why get over it, so that I can once again become a slave
Without identity and without history
Never can I simply "get over it"
But never will it be my excuse not to transcend

Lynches Poison

It's been way too many years and Willie Lynches poison still thrives here
We abide by the curse live expecting the worse
Were victimized and ostracized confused and mistreated
Confused because all traces of our past were deleted
They question this Letter's authenticity
But does this change the fact that everything on that letter is real and I'm still not free
By doubting its authenticity you try to hide the inhumane psychological mind games
That ensured that slavery is where my people would remain
Among my own people I'm ridiculed for my color
But before Master took liberties with the nigra women this was the color of your mother
Keep them separated by color and make one better than the other
We're enslaved to Willie's plan divide women from man
Feed them a lie and make them believe they need me to survive

You see we perm our hair to hide from our nappy roots
We live a lie because ignorance blocks the truth
We purposely marry outside our race to dismiss the features of our face
We neglect all traits that closely resemble our African ancestry
But divide and conquer was the mental psychology
The mental psychology used to keep my people bound
Forgetful of their past image still not found
Keeping this poison of ignorance flowing through my veins
This spirit of animosity that continuously reigns

See we were captured, beaten, rapped, robbed, and sold

Packed like sardines destination untold
Stripped of our culture made to live a lie
Abused in a way that can't even be denied
Sick tossed language lost the black Holocaust
Taught His Story pronounced history to believe we were inferior
Brutally lynching just to install the fear in ya
But in the midst of my struggle I had a dream
Sang spiritual hymns and worked as a team

Then we were fed drugs and sickness to continue to keep us bound
Forgetful of our past image still not found
School systems corrupt and again we're stuck
Lynching ourselves unconsciously enslaved
Raping, robbing, and beating, sending our own to their graves
Violence and crime taking over our streets, this poison we must defeat
Still divided why must we deny it
Still captured, beaten, rapped, robbed, and sold
Still fearful of our future destination untold
Now enslaved by the dollar drugs killing our future scholars
Fathers gone but by choice, Will you please hear my voice
We're still enslaved to Willie's plan divide women from man
Separated by color knowingly making one better than the other
We must stick together for we have come too far
To still be ignorant and uninformed of who we are
No longer will this poison flow through our veins
No longer will ignorance and animosity reign
No longer will there be division between you and me

Let us hang Lynches plan to a tree **and consider ourselves truly free**

Inspiration:
The World Through My Eyes:
Willy Lynch's Curse

I WAS INSPIRED to write the poem "Willy Lynch's Curse" after noticing the poison of ignorance, hate, and separation that continues to plague African Americans and blacks all over the world. In fact, this very same ignorance and separation is what creates issues worldwide. We are divided by race, religion, beliefs, political affiliation, sexual orientation, social background, age, class, and many other categories. This letter's authenticity has been highly questioned, but the point I make in this poem is that everything on that letter exists within the black race and is holding us in bondage. The techniques that the letter stated are used to make slaves are unquestionably alive and thriving. There was a strong amount of psychology used in order to break down the slaves and keep them ignorant. In this poem I discuss how this psychology is still greatly affecting the black race and how it is up to us to put the curse to bed.

In this poem I take the audience back to the way slaves were captured, beaten, raped, robbed, and sold. This was the beginning of the breaking and degrading of who we were. By taking the slaves from their homelands, raping their women, and robbing them of their culture, they were left without an identity. When they arrived in the New World, the only things the slaves had were their hope, their faith, and their souls. I believe this loss of identity is a strong factor in the issues of modern-day African Americans.

One of the strongest points I would like to make in this poem is how we were divided so that we could easily be conquered. This type of division plagues blacks worldwide. For example, the genocide in Rwanda was triggered by division. By dividing the slaves, it decreased their numbers because they were no longer one black race. If you closely evaluate this technique, you can see that it was most certainly used in the making of a slave, whether or not Lynch's letter was real. The slaves were divided by color and made to believe African features were wrong. The lighter the skin a slave was, the better they were treated . This same division plagues the black race today. Even in African American- based films, the role of the "pretty girl" is usually played by a lighter-skinned, usually bi-racial girl. This division must stop. We must unite and overcome our differences, because in all actuality, we will never overcome the struggle in separation.

My final point in this poem is how the poison has been placed, and that we are playing a great role in its development. We divide ourselves with different gangs and groups we place ourselves in. We feed the poison by allowing images of beauty to be based upon Western features. We feed the poison by bringing truth to certain stereotypes. We have come way too far to allow ourselves to be defeated by this poison that was set in us so long ago. As the human race, we must overcome our differences, break down barriers, and unite so that we can all grow as a race.

No More Lies

No more lies, please, no more lies
Keep my head in the books and my nose out of the sky
Open my eyes so that I can now realize
Stop teaching me things in school that are just theorized
Show me that someday everyone has to die
Stop feeding me these Fairy tale lies
Don't trick me into believing that there is a Santa Claus
Because he couldn't bring my best friend's life back when it came to a pause
Am I supposed to believe that being a minority makes me nothing at all
Please make actual African-American features when you change the color of a doll
I feel as if I'm surrounded by lies and deception
But now the truth lies in the youth and knowing the truth is a blessing
We don't have to live up to anyone's expectations
We are all beautiful because we're God's creations

So Many Tears

So many tears over so many years
I cried and I'm not even going to lie.
If Jesus did than why can't I.
The strongest man alive who didn't say a mumbling word, when he died.
Why should I hide emotions and feeling inside
Just another example of society trying to shape who I am.
There is only one person to walk the earth who is my example of a real man.
Some ladies say a good man is hard to find
Then it isn't love but the lover, who is blind.
Beg for a thug then cry because you can't get a hug.
Be careful of what you ask for because surely you might get
Just pray that it isn't something you will later regret.

Spiritual Warfare

It's a spiritual warfare and there's a prisoner of war here
Trying to fight this battle alone, and that's why I'm losing
The road to destruction is the one I'm choosing
My flesh has me oppressed, everyday is a test
Brain-washed and marching to the beat of this world, caught in a swirl
Conquered by temptation because my flesh lust, guess in God I didn't put all my trust
And now I'm guided by sin, ignoring the Jesus within
Envious because my eyes lust
Facing life after death when this **flesh** that **just, must, lust,** turns to **dust.**
And now I'm burning in the pit of eternal fire, without my worldly treasures
All because I oh so needed that fleshly pleasure

Who Are You?

Who are you to make someone feel a bit less than beautiful

Who are you to make someone feel a bit less than wonderful

Who are you to make someone cry? Who are you to kill their pride

Who are you to tell someone that they can't dress, who are you to impress

Who are you to tell someone that they are too fat or skinny

When you're probably nothing more than an envious enemy

Who are you to take advantage of another person's insecurity

When no one can actually fly like a butterfly and sting like a bee

Who are you to try to knock someone down to boost yourself up

Embarrass someone in a crowd like that is truly wasup

Who are you? You breathe the same air as I do

If making others feel bad makes you feel good

Then I have no respect **for you**

Double Minded

You see Lord one side of me wishes that I never knew you. I don't ever want to be held accountable for the things that I do.

This side of me wishes that I never went to church, or had a Christian family. I don't want to live by God's rules and commandments; I just want to live free.

Lord I don't want to have to face you on judgment day, and how do I know that there is a God anyway.

The bible says that to whom much is given much is required, and I know that I was given a lot so I'm just gonna try to forget it.

I am a double minded man therefore I am unstable in all of my ways. Maybe someday I'll choose you Lord, maybe one of these days.

At the same time I am confused because when Jesus speaks to my spiritual side he tells me that I can't run around saying someday because someday isn't promised, not even the next minute.

This spiritual side tells me that I just want to praise and exalt you. You have done so much for me in my life that when the fleshly side of me questions whether there is a God I know that you have to be true.

This battle is so fierce that I don't know who to choose. Wait! When I give it more thought my fleshly side just has to loose.

It is impossible to have two biological fathers, so how could I possibly have you and the devil as my fathers.

Heavenly Father when it all falls down satan has no power, no control, no dominion over me. Dear Lord I once was blind but now thanks to you I can see.
Now when I am faced with daily test and temptation and my fleshly being wants to attack, my spiritual side will just have to react, because I am no longer double minded and I am never going back.

You see living that worldly life I once felt free. Now someone please tell me how could that be. The Devil had me enslaved I was handcuffed to sin. Now I appreciate that Christian family who introduced me to the alpha, the omega, my best friend.

Counterfeit Christian

Jealousy and envy invade my mind
Although I sit in this pew and sip from this wine
Malicious thoughts and evil settle in my head
Although I sit in fellowship and eat from this bread
I want what you have because of the lust of my eyes
Although we all praise together, its you who I despise
I don't come to church because I want healing deep down inside
I come to look nice, and to nurture my pride
I appear to be holy because I'm here every Sunday
But no one really sees where I am every Monday
I cling to the numerically prospering church to feed my flesh
And besides there's just a few more heads to impress
I'm a counterfeit Christian but I appear to be holier than thou
But I only go as far as the church will allow

On A Mission Since
Conception!!!
Najee Carter
For
Class President
of
2007

The World Through My Eyes: On A Mission

The picture that you have just seen symbolizes my junior year in high school, which was a pivotal moment in my journey of knowledge, understanding, and personal growth. During this year, I made the bold and courageous decision to act on one of my dreams—becoming president of my senior class. My inspiration for making the decision to run for president was a famous quote by Mahatma Gandhi: "Be the change you wish to see in the world". This quotation empowered me to go for something that I have always wanted instead of only dreaming about it.

The decision to run for president would also prove challenging because of my newly developed friendship with the current president of my class. I wanted her to fully understand that my decision to run for president was in no way an attack on her, but only another stop on my mission of personal growth and development. I wanted everyone to understand that I was taking a stand in hopes that others would be inspired to do the same.

I came into the election the definite underdog. There were people who actually told me to my face that I wouldn't win, but I never let those statements discourage me. Although there were those who were obviously against me, I was extremely honored to know that I had people who supported me. I don't think those who supported me know exactly how important and appreciated it made me feel. It was a wonderful feeling to know that people trusted my ability to lead the senior class.

When hearing this story, many would like to hear that I won the election, but the reality is that I didn't. The day that I found out that I wouldn't be the next president hurt my soul. I didn't understand how a person could be disappointed time after time. I don't think anyone actually knew how I truly felt, because I had become accustomed to hiding my emotions in order to appear strong, but in actuality I was extremely hurt.

I strongly believe that everything happens for a reason, and this truly did. When I came home I told my mom the outcome of the election with a smile on my face in an attempt to hide the way I was truly feeling, but I couldn't hide my emotions for long. I thank my mother for making me feel like a winner when I felt like I was less than a person. She told me how proud she was that I had even made the decision to run for president. I—the shy boy who was very fearful of others' opinions—made the decision to run for president in a class of more than four hundred.. That day I was also greeted with balloons and a card from my grandmother, who congratulated me as if I had won; in her eyes, I had.

I would later come to understand my accomplishments. I made the decision to be the change that I wanted to see. This experience helped me grow as a person. I faced doubt, betrayal, injustice, and many other obstacles, and I came out a stronger and wiser person. If I had actually won that election, I would have never learned that sometimes you have to reach deep inside to see that you are a winner when the world tells you that you are not. After that experience, I was able to continue on my mission as a stronger and wiser young man, ready to face a world that has very negative views. That makes me a winner.

I Can Now Fly

I have finally let go of everything that once held me down
I can finally see clearly because the rain is now gone
I will now spread my wings and fly into the future
Achieving all of my goals and fulfilling all of my dreams
Going as far as my mind will take me
I will march to the beat of my own drum
And can't anyone rain on my parade
I will be a success story and I dare someone to fly with me
To let go of all the pain and soar
I dare somebody to shine with me
I dare you to be the superstar that you are
Just let go and Fly

New Beginnings
The Beginning Of A New Man

Goodbye immaturity for I am older now
Goodbye jealousy and the weights that once held me down
Goodbye insecurity for I have learned to love me
Goodbye childish ways for I am wiser now with days
Goodbye petty fights, fear, and tearful nights
Goodbye to lust for in God I now trust
Goodbye to pride for I have true comfort inside
Goodbye deceitful lies for I have now found truth
Goodbye expectations as I slowly leave my youth

Goodbye being phony for I now have a true testimony
Goodbye puppy love for I now put him first
Good bye to excuses and that generational curse
Goodbye to that follower for I now lead
Goodbye envy, lust, pride, and greed
Goodbye evil and demons that plague my mind
Goodbye to procrastination and wasting my time
Goodbye to mama's arms for I must now stand on my own

Hello to peace within my mind as I journey away from home
Hello to freedom, respect, and dignity
Hello to truth, love, and honesty
Hello to the realization that everyday is a test
Hello to appreciation and knowing that I am blessed
Hello to wisdom for I have come a long way
Hello to happiness, joy, and a brand new day
Hello to hope and positivity
Hello to the embracement of my sensitivity
Hello to comfort, assertiveness, and confidence

Hello to healing, forgiveness, and repentance
Hello to courage and integrity
Hello to the beginning of a brand new Me!

Voice Of The Ghetto

Ghetto by birth and not by choice
Will someone acknowledge my unheard voice?
Born in America ignored by its elite
Intelligence and creativity trapped in the streets
Trying to carry on in a world filled with greed
What you fail to realize is that like you I bleed
Like you I lament and like you I cry
Unplug your ears and hear the whole ghettoes sigh

Hungry children, neglect, and welfare checks
Broken souls, loneliness, unprotected sex
Drug-dealers dealing and appealing to the crack addict
Appearing to be charismatic but love he never had it
It's systematic this struggle its problematic this hustle
Keeping your head above water you can't ignore this self slaughter
Born in poverty for you to further demolish me
Denied of my education to ease your frustration
Ghetto by birth and not by choice
Will someone acknowledge my unheard voice?

Single mothers struggling childhood cut short
Father not ready so she takes him to court
He gives child support but that's not what the child needs
He needs someone to teach him, show him, and lead
He needs someone to trust and to direct him to manhood
She needs a father to love her and to tell her she looks good
Surely that rapist, molester, or even cereal-killer would
Ghetto by birth and not by choice
Will someone hear my unheard voice?

For all my people in the ghetto in the states and world-wide
Stay steady, determined, and hopeful keeping the faith alive
When the road seems dreary and journey too long
Hold your head high love yourself and stay strong
Within the youth of the ghetto lies hope
 The future is in our hands
Young men stand up take your place and be a man
Young women stay strong and receive the respect you demand
To the child that feels hopeless and lonely
Without a test there is no testimony
To the young thug hustling you're our future entrepreneurs and mathematicians
The enemy would have you feel like you were nothing to keep you from your mission
To all the single mothers stay strong and continue the fight
To the gang bangers fight for a cause and unite
Too all those in the ghetto blinded from the light
I just want you to know that everything is going to be alright
Ghetto by birth victorious by choice

Eventually someone will acknowledge my **voice**

Victim Of The Streets

He was an eighteen-year-old victim lying on the streets.

I couldn't help but notice that his shoes were gone from his feet.

Blood covered the scene and the young man was dead.

They said that he took four bullets to the chest and one to the head.

I got the opportunity to speak to him before he passed;

I saw the hurt in his face; and the emotions in his eyes, I read.

Then he told me his life story, and this is what he said:

Why Kill What We Made

It was January 23, 1987, one of the coldest days of the year. The weather was brutal. There was snow, sleet, and ice-covered roads. My parents had gotten into a fight because my mom was three months pregnant with their fourth child. That child was me—Isaiah Smith. My father didn't want another child because he couldn't financially support the three he already had. I'm not making a decision for other women, but my mom strongly disagreed with abortion. "Why kill what you made?" was her argument. My father completely ignored my mom's opinion and told her that if she didn't have an abortion, he would kill her. These were extremely harsh words, but his selfish tendencies led him to feel this way. I didn't ask to be in this world. It wasn't my decision. When Mom refused to have an abortion, my father beat her. He beat her as if she were a slave who refused to listen to her master. Momma was sent to the hospital that night. Doctors didn't know if she would make it, but both my mother and I are survivors. On July 18, 1987, I was born.

Grandma's House

After leaving my father, Momma went to live with my grandmother on Smith Street in Newark, New Jersey. We lived there for eight years. I spent eight years of my life not knowing who my father was or whether I was supposed to have one. I thought that it was natural for your mother and grandmother to raise you. I loved my grandmother. She was everything that a grandmother should be: kind, sweet, loving, and generous. She also saved me from a few butt whippings. We stayed with her while Mom worked two jobs. Mom's daytime job was at the post office, but we never knew what her night job was. All we knew was that the majority of the money went to her schooling.

When I turned six years old, my grandmother was extremely ill. Although she didn't like the idea, staying at a nursing home was the best decision for her. My two oldest siblings took on the parental roles. My sister, Monica, at the age of twelve, would make sure that the house was clean and that we were fed. Monica was always very independent and strongly opinionated. Tyrone, who was the oldest, was always very deviant.

He was responsible for watching over us and making sure we were safe. Tyrone was always extremely popular and greatly respected. He was well known for being a great fighter. Not that that's the most honorable thing. He would always bully me, but if anyone else tried to hurt me, he was there to protect me. My other brother is named Jamal. He can pretty much be described as a follower. He always wanted to be like Tyrone or the other people in the neighborhood who weren't exactly positive role-models.

I was usually the well-behaved child. I was always very intelligent. I was placed in the second grade straight from kindergarten. Being the youngest of four most certainly never got me any extra attention. Between Mom working and Tyrone being punished, I was rarely noticed.

Education and Basketball

I attended Lincoln Avenue Elementary School. In my early days, I excelled in school. I guess education was always for me. By the time I was eight years old, I was in the fourth grade. Because of my older brother's status, I had many friends and few enemies. I also excelled on the basketball court. I always played basketball with my brother and his friends. Playing with the older guys made me extremely competitive. I never took losing easily, so I played extra hard to win. After I got home from school each day, I would eat lunch, do my homework, and play basketball at the school playground. I developed this routine while my grandmother was home, but when she became ill, homework was slowly eliminated from the routine. I had no one to make sure I was doing homework. Nobody was there to help me or even to check my homework. Monica was too busy on the phone, and Jamal and Tyrone were hanging out with friends, so I was free to make my own decisions. Do you know what would later evolve from this freedom? The 'hood would become my playground, and drugs my toys. My teachers became worried about my missing homework. They also questioned the way I was dressed. Since I dressed myself, I would come to school in shorts in the middle of the winter. I was my own man; I had to fend for myself. Mom worked two jobs to keep the family alive, and my father was missing in action. Mom did the best she could as a mother, but she had to have money to financially support us. I loved my mom, and I honored her for her strength. For a person to raise children on his or her own is incredible. I feel that it takes two to make a child, and that therefore, two should raise that child. I promised myself that when I have children, it would be with someone I truly love and care for. It is unfair for a child to be born into a terrible situation that he or she didn't even ask for.

While I let education slide, basketball was still my passion. I was inspired by Michael Jordan, Allen Iverson, Charles Barkley, and Shaq. Unfortunately, I didn't have a dad to play ball with me or teach me the basics. I didn't know the impact that growing up without a father would have on me, but it scarred me for life.

It's So Hard To Say Goodbye

When I was eight years old, the most disastrous thing happened to me: My mom passed away. I didn't understand why she would leave me in this world all alone. I loved her with all of my soul. My mom embodied dignity and strength. I love her for the morals and values that she taught me. They say all good things must come to an end, but the reality of death was devastating. This was the first, but most certainly not the last, death I would see. In the 'hood, death is a natural occurrence. Besides the memories my mom left me, I found her favorite gold chain. I wore that chain so that it would be adjacent to my heart. I promised myself that no matter what happened, I would never let the chain go. I was heartbroken after the death of my mom. I kept silent for a whole month. I had no other family besides my grandmother, who was extremely ill, so my siblings and I had to be sent to foster homes. Nothing was making sense to me. First, I lost the most important person to me. Second, I was being separated from my brothers and my sister. What is death? Why does it happen? Why do we live to die? These are questions that I asked myself over and over again. Just like I didn't ask to come into this world, I'm sure Mom didn't ask to leave it. Being away from my loved ones felt like being in solitary confinement. It felt like I had been abandoned and left to survive in this cruel world all alone. I learned that I must value those whom I love while they're living so that when they pass, I won't have guilt to add to the sorrow. Before my mom passed, I disobeyed her. She wanted me to start doing my homework, but instead I went straight to the playground. I didn't disobey her often, so I thought that one time wouldn't hurt her. Instead, it hurt me for the rest of my life. I wondered what life was like after death. If living is so hard, then death must be simple. It's so hard to say goodbye to someone you loved and admired. I saw my mom's passion and admired it. She worked hard to keep our family alive.

She had dreams of getting out of the ghetto. Mom wanted much more for her kids. In my heart, I felt lonely and confused. I felt isolated from the world. The day I left my brothers and my sister hurt me like a billion tuberculosis shots entering my flesh. A part of me was already empty from not having a father figure; now my heart was broken.

In the next portion of my life, I was sent to a series of foster homes. I ran away most of the times, wishing I could find The Wiz so he could send me back home. When I was eleven years old, I was finally adopted by a lady I strongly disliked. Her presence made me shiver. She had a face that always expressed anger. She was in her mid-thirties. Her name was Mrs. Williams. She never allowed me to call her Mom—not that I even wanted to. She was always jealous of me because she knew it was inevitable that my future would be bright. Her three sons, however, were all knuckleheads. They bullied me, but Tyrone wasn't there to save me anymore. When Mrs. Williams whipped me, grandma wasn't there to talk her out of it. This life was miserable. I felt like Annie; it was definitely a hard-knock life for me. Mrs. Williams never showed me love. My broken heart never came close to being repaired.

While playing outside, I would see many things that seemed natural to me. I would see gangs, drug dealers, crack addicts, and gang violence. The drug dealers became my idols. They drove the best cars, had the most beautiful women, and wore the best clothes. That wealth, to me, symbolized success. It didn't matter to me that it was illegal. I had already learned that you have to take the good with the bad. This street life, which was glorified in rap videos, was my life. I was a child of the ghetto. The gang member represented strength. This strength was much different from the strength Mom possessed. This strength was physical. I had learned from watching the Discovery Channel that only the strong survive, so I wanted to become strong. I thought that my mom's strength wasn't enough, since she didn't survive.

Mrs. Williams never bought me any nice toys or clothes. On Christmas, I literally got a bag of coal. So I started to sell drugs at thirteen. From then on, I always had the hottest clothes and the best sneakers. This made the other guys envy me and the ladies love me. Every day I entered middle school, I was fresh to death. It gave me a strong feeling of confidence to be the best-dressed guy in school. This life of easy money was something that I could live with.

As humans, we have a habit of wanting things quick, fast, and in a hurry. We want our money, food, cars, and even our women fast. The moral thing to do would be to work hard for things that you want, but getting them easily felt so much better. Now when I look back over my life, I wish that I would have never become content in my own laziness. If my ancestors had to struggle for the very freedom I have, why should I throw it away as if their sweat, blood, and tears meant nothing to me. Being young and naive, I never even considered the possibility of being arrested. I was arrested by the illusion that I was just a ghetto boy from the streets who didn't have a future. Despite my intelligence and my drive, seeing the people around me led me to believe that there was no such thing as a better life. I had many dreams and aspirations, but I put them all aside to receive the pleasure of the present. I had already placed the past behind me without even considering my future. I still had dreams of going to the NBA, but for now this money was looking right. This is where I wanted to be. Since the ghetto is always glorified, I was proud to be from the hood. At thirteen I was making more money than Mrs. Williams. It just couldn't get any better. I wish that I would have recognized that this wasn't the life for me. Being a thug or a gangster just wasn't who I am.

Mom always told me that I would be the college graduate, the successful entrepreneur, and the honorable family man. I was compromising who I was for a life that wasn't for me. When I look at the many young men who turn to a life of hustling to survive, I understand them. It is so easy to judge people without taking a walk in their shoes. The gang member is often times a young boy who has no father or mother; he feels that the gang is a shelter and a place of security for him. The quick money that comes with selling drugs is something they've never seen before. If everyone were granted equal education and shown that there are other ways of making money, maybe they would try harder to be successful. If we had more positive role-models in the ghettoes, we would strive to be like them. For the person who has never had anything; money, power, and women are beautiful things to have.

Later in life I found out that Mom's night job was exotic dancing. In other words, she was a stripper. Also, my mom didn't just simply pass away, she was murdered. They say the strong survive, but does that pertain to the mentally strong? It has to, because even though my mom isn't physically alive, she still lives. She lives within my soul; therefore, she is a survivor. One night after getting off of work late, my mom refused to have sex with a man, so he raped her and then stabbed her to death. I don't understand how someone could take a person's life. I would wish anything but death upon a person. Death affects a person's friends and family. Death affected me. Learning that my mom had been murdered shattered my already broken heart.

School, To Me, Wasn't Cool

By my sophomore year, I was doing a mediocre job in school. I could easily pass a quiz or test, but I wasn't doing the homework and projects. I maintained Cs and Bs. I knew if Mom had been around, she wouldn't have liked my grades; but If I had known what her night job was, I wouldn't have liked that either. Some may ask why my mom would have even considered an occupation so degrading to women if she was so strong. I would simply answer them by saying that she had to feed her family. I clearly understood why Mom had the job she did, but I used it as an excuse for me to sell drugs. I had to look nice, of course; that was the approach of the ignorant and young boy that I once was. I would do homework every now and then just to ensure that I wasn't failing. I believe that Mrs. Williams liked to see that I wasn't putting all of my effort into school. She never told me to do homework or improve my grades. She had an extremely envious heart.

I hadn't actually joined a gang, but I was closely associated with one by the time I was sixteen years old.

Being surrounded by these individuals gave me a sense of security, but deep inside, I was afraid. I was afraid of this world that took my mother and everything that I ever loved from me. I was afraid that I could be the next victim of the streets. I wish that I would have known that these people did not care for me as a person and did not have my best interest at heart. I was only a game to them. I was a naive young boy who could easily be fooled and controlled. The absence of a mother and father in my life made me vulnerable to their deception and their illusion of protection.

During my senior year in high school, I made the foolish decision to drop out. I was lost and confused. I was merely another statistic, living a life that would surely lead me to death. I had become a ruthless individual. Putting on this façade of strength was my way of protecting myself against this cruel world. I knew no other way of protection.

I felt foolish for allowing myself to fall victim to the wrongdoings of the world I was living in. I didn't realize that education was what would free me and keep me from being ignorant and uninformed of the world around me. Education is highly important to an African-American male in a world that expects him to fail. If I could set a goal, it would be to not give the world the satisfaction of seeing me fail in life. This point of my life was the ultimate low. I degraded myself and allowed myself to be devoured by the world. I was an emotional wreck with no sense of direction.

Tomorrow Is Not Promised

The passing of my grandmother was a turning point in my life. I couldn't cope with yet another great loss. I never even got the chance to say goodbye to the women I loved so dearly. Now I was truly alone. I felt I was lost and without an identity. I knew that deep down inside, the life I was living was wrong. I knew that my grandmother could never rest in peace knowing that I threw away all of the morals and knowledge that she gave me.

I had dreams and goals that I never accomplished. I insisted on procrastinating as if tomorrow were promised. It was hard to even think about a brighter future during a time when clouds of darkness rained heavily on me. The storm seemed as if it would never be over. One day while reflecting on my past and all of the obstacles I faced, I decided that it was time to make a change. I decided that I would finally go for all of my dreams. I also decided to not let my past dictate my future.

He then left, and looking at the smile on his face put joy in my head.

The next time I saw this young man, he was on the news, but he was dead.

I fell in my bed and cried so many tears.

This young man has been through it all in just a few short years.

They wanted his gold chain, but when he refused, they shot him again and again.

He seemed like a good kid, and I hope that heaven is where his soul will go.

I just want everyone out there to know: stay focused, and reach for your goals.

This short story is my way of expressing sympathy to victims of the streets. During the previous year, there have been many deaths among the youth living in the inner city. Those people who lost their lives died with dreams. It saddens me to know that people were unable to fulfill their dreams because of the ignorance that haunts our inner-city streets. I want this short story to inspire people to learn from the past in order to create a better future.

The Supposed Oppressor

If I speak intelligently then I'm no longer considered black
So am I supposed to be ignorant and uneducated, violent and defiant?
No. Because I don't meet others at there level instead I transcend
Envious minds while still blaming the oppressor consider me an uppity Negro
Still blaming the supposed oppressor, but the oppressor is you
Comfortable in your predicament too lethargic to rise
Insinuating that I've compromised because I don't continue to allow myself to be victimized
Accepting an image of ignorance while alienating those who are successful
Afraid of success so you're afraid to try your best
Degrading women, abandoning children and still blaming the supposed oppressor for your failures
Afraid to recognize that you are your biggest oppressor
Frowning down upon education while idolizing material things
Intelligent entrepreneurial minds misguided into the life of illegal hustling
Only awaiting their early death, because they feel that's the only way
Dreams that people don't believe are tangible are instead abandoned
Saddened and distraught minds violently taking lives
Fooled to believe they're displaying strength, but truly their emotionally unstable
Taking lives believing they have nothing to live for
While still blaming the supposed oppressor
Broken homes leaving their children to be raised by the streets
Young girls allowing themselves to be exploited and Momma still puts total blame on the videos,

but a house built on a weak foundation will fall when the wolf blows
Unsafe streets, school systems insufficient, people taking lives, still afraid to rise
And I realize that if you aren't the solution then you are the problem
The oppressor is you because you chose to be oppressed
While placed in this world with disadvantages,
It's still your choice to allow yourself to remain oppressed
Denying education while condoning ignorance and postponing success
The sums of education and knowledge are freedom and power
With education being available you allow yourself to be oppressed, while still blaming the supposed oppressor

My Mission

My main goal and purpose for writing this book is to at least inspire one person to better themselves and to live their dreams regardless of any obstacles they may face. I am a living success story. I have battled low self-esteem, feelings of inadequacy, and even depression. On this day I can honestly say that I am here and that the storm is over now. Although the journey was far from easy I am living proof that anything is possible if you only have the faith. When I had reached rock bottom and felt like there was no place to go I handed my troubles over to God.

As people we tend to be hard headed. As one human-being I am not equipped to fight a battle so fierce all alone and I don't have to. After I have done all that I could, there was nothing left to do but to stand. The only thing that I had to do was to believe. Simply believe. Some may ask how could I have faith in something that I couldn't see. Faith is the substance of things hoped for and the evidence of things **not yet seen.** I had the faith and that is why I am still here today. No psychological treatment could have given me the strength that I now have.

Upon discovering my gift of poetry I also found that my art form was therapeutic. It would be selfish of me to keep my gift for my own personal healing. I have been on a mission from the time I set foot on this earth. I now realize that satan has planted these insecurities in me to keep me from my mission but I am here. I am here to be strong for anyone who has ever been oppressed, for anyone who has ever felt inadequate. I want you to know that when you believe in God and he gives you the strength to believe in yourself, there is nothing that could keep you from fulfilling your destiny. For everyone who has a dream go for it. I would rather have been disappointed a thousand times then to die without ever attempting to pursue my dreams. For anyone whose ability has been doubted, use that negativity as the fuel to keep you determined and motivated. Finally when finished reading my book I ask that you take a moment and think. Think about where and what you want to be in the next five years and go for it. **Never give up on your dreams.**

I Am The Future

I am the future so today I take a stand
My wisdom and love will spread across this land
Yesterday has passed and today is God's gift
Tomorrow is just another day for me to spiritually uplift
Broken souls wanting to be free
I am the future and the future is me

I will grow from the trials and mistakes of my past
I will make a promise to never finish last
I will pour my soul into everything I do
I will work hard to see that my dreams come true
 I will make a vowel to be all that I can be
I am the future and the future is me

I am the future and I am the truth
I am the hope for a better world because I am the youth
I will be the one to further my education
Thinking with my heart and teaching through demonstration
I will be the change that I wish to see
I am the future and the future is me

Can I

Can I be your inspiration
Can you learn from my determination
Can my love spread throughout the nation
Can I be the seed that grows, Can I be the light that glows
Can I be Sojourner's truth, Can I be the voice of the youth

Can I be your motive to succeed
Can I be your inspiration to take the lead
Can I be your vision in the night, Or like a shooting star shining bright
Can I be the soul that lives within, Can I be what lies underneath your skin
Can I show you faith that won't end, Can I be your motive to try again

Can I be your freedom and liberty
Can I be the cure to your every insecurity
Can I be the wisdom that you gain, Can I be the healer of your pain
Can I be your strength when you're weak or your voice when you can't speak
Can I be your wealth when you feel poor, Can I be the dream that you're fighting for
I Can

You
(No One In Your Corner)

When you think there is no one in your corner
The sky looks bleak
Because the sun has not been told to shine
and the water is controlling the moon as it seems to tiptoe around
causing your attitude to flip flop between full, half, and quarter
You feel unexplainable then you drift off to a place where no
One is allowed to go
There you can commune with the father knowing that just a little talk with Jesus
will make it all right
Now you can continue to be all that God ordained you to be

I want you to know all is not lost
Jesus did not hang suffer and die on the cross
For you to be lost
It was for a reason and that reason is you
Yes you

If you have any doubt let me clear your mind
You were wonderfully made because
you are the handy work of God almighty
You are so loved by the most high
Who is always making provision to carry you along the way
Sending angles along your journey
With messages to keep you focused
The protector to bring to your remembrance all that you need to know

While the enemy tried to block your direction

He drops boulders in your path but
God crushes them into pebbles
He rolls out a blanket of sand for you to trod upon

Its so great to know him but even better for him to know you..
Gee You will always have my love even when I am not around to give it.

Love Mama

To My Oldest Son, Najee

To My oldest son, Najee K. Carter: It is my pleasure to witness your celebration and embracement of self. For so long I wanted to protect you from the ways of this world, but I always knew you would have to one day face it all alone. I must say that I am quite pleased with your outcome. I often say I can't wait until you go to college, but as the time quickly approaches, it is a feeling of not being able to be a part of your every day life that frightens me.

I have often tried to make you comfortable with yourself. It was not until I personally had the opportunity to read your work that I was forced to revisit some things that I was not comfortable with about my self. You are so right; loving Christ first and then loving oneself is the only way to teach others to love. You are my son, and I simply adore you.

Being a young mother, I have had to learn along the way, but I pray that I have not done anything that will affect your life in a negative way. I remember one day when you were about fifteen years old and you were crying after a discussion we had. I asked you what was wrong. I was not prepared for what you said next. You said, "Mom, I don't think you love me." I thought to myself before I even answered you, *only satan could be so crafty as to confuse you and lie to you.* Well, I told you then and I am telling you now that I love you more than life. I have no favorites, you each—meaning, Najee, Omar, and Khari—bring a different joy into my life. I love you so much, Najee, that no amount of words could begin to express the way I feel. I thank God for your accomplishment, and remember: You can do whatever you set your mind to. Just always remember to give credit to the Lord and Savior Jesus Christ. Allow him to direct your path. To the parents, not knowing what clouds your children's heads is a battle. Sometimes they don't feel they can discuss things with us. That is a scary thing because it forces them to internalize things that, if not expressed, could end in tragedy. So, Najee, I love you. You're handsome, you're great, but most of all, you're a child of the most high king of kings, Jesus Christ. The world is yours. God Bless.

PS Najee, you have always carried the weight of the world on your shoulders, always concerned about my life and wanting to protect me. I am living for my children and I will never regret the sacrifices that I have made.

Love Mom

Innocent Child Left

Innocent child left all alone
Dysfunctional family no father at home
Educated by the streets
Ignorance is what he meets
Fed lies called stereotypes meant to keep him down
Morals and love nowhere to be found
Deceived by his peers, stupidity growing with years
Drug dealing like it's a game, behavior inhumane
Pride longing for recognition, he calls it his hustler's ambition
Joined a gang couldn't bang but figured he hang
Felt so secure how immature
He thought that was his family
Because they were there to hide his fears and nurture his insecurities
But when he got arrested his thoughts were tested cuz once again he was alone
But this time there was no home
So the streets were his to roam
Blind leading the blind led by radio and TV
Like Ray Charles leading Stevie but believe it wasn't easy
How long will this stupidity reign?
When will he realize that God gave him a brain?
How much lies and deception can one body contain?
How much hurt and pain can one soul sustain?
Will he ever claim victory over greed or is he the contaminated seed?

See he was told if he sold he could live the fast life
Abundance of money, extravagant cars, crazy sex but no wife
Just a shorty he called his jump off
 Who was self-conscious enough to jump off when he told her

He said he needed a weight lift off his shoulder
Mom dukes went ballistics when he told her
So she sat down and prayed with him and at that very moment the spirit saved him
And that young man was me careless but in no way free
Conquered by greed the contaminated seed
But I had to make the decision to be the seed to conquer greed
Proceed and take the lead! And I ain't turning back

The Parents Pledge

I Promise to make my home a safe haven.
I Promise to refrain from the use of any derogatory language or profanity when speaking to my children.
I promise to reward and compliment my child instead of constantly reminding him/her of negativity.
I promise to embrace my child on a daily basis with love and affection.
I promise to deal with my own insecurities so that I do not pass them down from generation to generation.
I promise to stand behind a child who dares to be different, and encourage him/her to love them selves and to remember that God made them **special**.
Remember Parents, each generation should be better than the last. Let us together as a community, as a race, as a culture, as a world break down the chains of insecurity, self- hatred, violence etc. Let's stop instilling rejection, in the form of absentee mothers or fathers, Let us break the generational curses and replace them with a positive movement.
Let's start right here, right now today.
We are responsible for the world we live in today.

I promise: _____
      Date: _____
Name (child): _____

The Pledge of the Youth

My poetry has allowed me to develop and mature as a person. I am no longer that insecure young man afraid of his own greatness. I now understand that low self-esteem was only an obstacle in life that I had to overcome in order to fulfill my dreams and to be the best person I could be. There was a point in my life when I decided that I needed to take that journey to find my inner strength. I am now learning to love every single portion of me. I challenge everyone to take that same journey. I want everyone to take a moment and close their eyes to think about everything that I have spoken about. I would like for you to think with your heart and allow yourself to heal from anything that has kept you away from fulfilling your goals.

I, Najee K. Carter, challenge anyone who is inwardly dealing with any type of depression, low self-esteem, or simply feeling as if they don't fit into the world's view of perfect to find out who they are. Look into the mirror every single day and embrace a different part of you. Don't allow the love to stop at the physical things because it is important to love and understand the soul underneath your skin.

You might be a singer, writer, dancer, actor, surgeon, lawyer, teacher even the next president of the United States. We were all put on this earth with talents it is up to you to find them. My gift came in the art form of writing and It has helped me to begin to see that in this world being different is a plus not a negative.

- I promise to learn to love every portion of me
- I promise to not compromise who I am
- I promise to remain truthful to myself and to those around me
- I promise to compliment myself each and every day
- I promise to stand strong in the midst of a storm
- I promise to hold my head high and to remain confident
- I promise to not fear my own greatness
- I promise to be more than what stereotypes and statistics make me
- I promise to keep God first

Name _____ Date _____

1 Luv, N. Carter

Please feel free to contact me and share your thoughts at
onamission2007@aol.com

Time Out To Meet The Author

NAJEE KHABIR CARTER was born to Tangela Monique Brown and Tyrone Lynn Carter on August 3, 1989 In Columbus Hospital in Newark, N.J. He weighed 6lbs and 13oz. Who would have known that this would be the beginning of his Mission Statement? At the time of his birth we lived in Newark, New Jersey

When Najee was of school age he attended Lincoln Ave School in Vailsburg New Jersey. After graduating the 5th grade we moved to South Center Street in Orange. There he attended Lincoln Ave School, following graduation Najee went on to Orange Middle School. He later transferred to Our Lady Help of Christians Academy in East Orange for 7th and 8th grades. We moved to Bloomfield. There he attended Bloomfield High School where he has put his stamp on the map never to be forgotten by his many friends and peers.

Najee will be graduating in June of 2007 and plans to go on to college and major in Journalism. His past times consist of studying, writing, being on the computer, hanging with like minded friends, and enjoying life's simple things. Najee has been on a mission since Conception and there is no stopping him. This will not be the last time you will hear from him, So Sit back and enjoy the ride. God Bless.

Printed in the United States
78063LV00003B/301-999